A Letter to
Solomon

Illustrated by
Dylan B. Caleho

Written by
Mari Shaw

Published by
The Galleries at Moore College of Art & Design

Copyright © 2022, Mari Shaw

THE CORONAVIRUS IS HERE!

Two months after the Coronavirus outbreak, Grandma Mari wrote a letter to her 10 year old grandson Solomon, "This virus is the most earth-shattering experience that has happened in your lifetime. But I am optimistic that many of us will learn from this frightening and uncertain time what is important and become better and wiser people. I know you will, my dear Solomon. It is so lonely for you not to be with your friends, your teammates, you teachers and your coaches. To help you get through this strange, scary time, I will write you a letter every day.

Every day after his virtual classes, Solomon rushed down the stairs to find the letter from Grandma Mari. On cold or rainy days, he cuddled his dog Daisy and read Grandma M's letter in his room. When the weather was fine, Solomon ran into his backyard, climbed his favorite tree, nestled in a seat of branches and read Grandma M's letter. Solomon laughed when his Grandma wrote about their imaginary adventures.

"Remember when we dressed as superheroes and summoned our radioactive powers to defeat the bad guys? Or when we wore our astronaut costumes to pilot our spaceship high into the sky? Or when we snuck through the night searching for thieves, evil geniuses, and ancient treasures."

Solomon found comfort and courage in his Grandma's letters. And the memories Grandma M described of their fun together aroused his imagination.

Solomon always answered his Grandma's letters. He wrote about playing his snare drums, what he was reading and his progress in teaching his dog Daisy to obey, count with her paws and talk with her barks. If Grandma sent Solomon a book, art supplies or sports equipment, Solomon slipped a poem or a picture in his thank you letter.

¡EL CORONAVIRUS YA ESTÁ AQUÍ!

Desde que empezó el Coronavirus, Soloman bajaba corriendo las gradas cuando acababan las clases virtuales a ver si le llego una carta de su abuelita Mari. Cuando llegaba la carta en días fríos y lluviosos, Solomon se acurrucaba con su perrita Daisy en su cuarto y leía la carta. Si el clima era bueno, Solomon corría al patio y leía su carta acurrucado en las ramas altas de su árbol favorito.

Solomon se reía cuando la abuelita escribía sobre sus aventuras imaginarias. "¿Recuerdas cuando éramos superhéroes y usábamos nuestros poderes radioactivos para eliminar a nuestros enemigos? ¿O cuando usábamos nuestros disfraces de astronautas para pilotear nuestras naves espaciales en lo alto del cielo? ¿O cuando nos vestíamos como espías que se escabullen en la noche y buscaban ladrones, genios malvados y tesoros antiguos?"

La abuelita Mari a menudo le hacía acuerdo a Solomon que "nunca olvides el poder de la magia" para ayudar a consolarlo durante el tiempo extraño e impredecible. Como agradecimiento, Solomon siempre respondía las cartas de su abuelita. Y si la abuelita Mari le enviaba un regalo para sorprenderlo (un libro, equipo deportivo o artículos de arte), Solomon le ponía un poema o un dibujo en su carta de agradecimiento.

A pesar de la distancia entre ellos y un futuro incierto, la conexión entre un niño y su abuelita pudo brindar un nivel de confianza y diversión.

Fly your own flag - brave knight.
What is your kingdom's name?

Flamea tu propia bandera - valiente caballero.
¿Cuál es el nombre de tu reino?

You could put on an art show, just like the famous Frida Kahlo!

Tú podrías exhibir tu arte, como la famosa Frida Kahlo.

Playing with friends can still be fun with a mask.

Jugandao con tus amigos puede ser divertido con mascarilla.

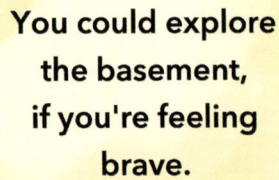

You could do nothing at all.

O podrías hacer nada en absoluto.

GRANDMA MARI WAS RIGHT!

When Grandma Mari promised Solomon that the horrors of the Coronavirus would pass, she was right.

Schools are open. Recess is back. Kids are playing with their friends without masks. Sports teams are going strong. When Solomon and his friends meet up to bike, skateboard, or shoot baskets, they can once again go inside stores to buy snacks with money they earned from weeding lawns or from their lemonade stand. Solomon is dreaming and creating bigger than ever: writing stories, drawing imaginary monsters and heroes, building and inventing new and amazing things.

Just as Grandma Mari predicted, the Coronavirus taught Solomon what is important. Solomon will never again complain about going to school, scrubbing his hands or getting vaccinated. Nor will he ever forget the kindness and generosity of his family, friends, teachers, coaches and neighbors. Daisy too! Always there, wagging her tail, happy to see him, and hoping he would take her out for a walk.

Solomon will always remember, after everyone in his family was vaccinated and the Coronavirus settled down, the first time he saw Grandma Mari's mask-free smiling face, the big hug she gave him before following him upstairs to see how he had rearranged his room and the current projects he was working on. Just as she did when he was a little kid, Grandma M. tickled Solomon until he begged her to stop.

Thank you for reading.

OUR TEAM

This book was a team effort, and would not have been possible without the talented group of passionate contributors and The Galleries at Moore College of Art & Design. Heartfelt thanks to:

Dylan B. Caleho - Illustrator, colorist, and master drafter whose vision truly made this story come to life.

Matt Kalasky - Editor and project manager whose suggestions, instincts, and long history with Moore brought this book and team together.

Maria Luisa Salazar and Steph Weigner - Artists and Moore alumna who helped by providing Spanish translations and coloring assistance, respectively, for this book.

Gabrielle Lavin Suzenski - Director of The Galleries at Moore College of Art & Design. The powerhouse who kept us on schedule, and saw to the book's being published in record time.

And a great big hug and kiss to dear Solomon, whose laughter, imagination, and kindness cures whatever ails me.

- Mari Shaw aka Grandma Mari

Este libro fue hecho con el esfuerzo de un gran equipo de talentosos y apasionados colaboradores y Moore College of Art & Design que sin ellos estono hubiera sido posible. Muchísimas gracias a:

Dylan B Caleho - Nuestra ilustrador, colorista, y maestra dibujante cuya visión realmente hizo que esta historia cobrará vida.

Matt Kalasky- Editor y director de proyecto cuyas sugerencias, instintos y conexiones con Moore unieron este libro y al equipo.

Maria Luisa Salazar y Steph Weigner- Artistas y ex alumnos de Moore que proporcionaron las traducciones al español y la asistencia para colorear, respectivamente, para este libro.

Gabrielle Lavin Suzenski- Directora de las Galerías en Moore College of Art & Design, quien nos mantuvo progresando según loplaneado y se encargó de que el libro se publicará en un tiempo récord.

Y un gran beso y abrazo al querido Solomon, cuya risa, imaginacióny amabilidad curan cualquier dolencia.

- Mari Shaw aka Abuelita Mari